S0-EDQ-825

Legal LUNACY

Unbelievable but True Laws— Past and Present!

by Anne and Tom Condon

Illustrations by Rick Penn-Kraus

PRICE STERN SLOAN
Los Angeles

Copyright 1992 by Anne and Tom Condon
Published by Price Stern Sloan, Inc.
11150 Olympic Boulevard
Los Angeles, California 90064
Printed in U.S.A.

10 9 8 7 6 5 4 3 2 1

All rights reserved. No part of this publication may be reproduced, stored in a retrieval system or transmitted in any form or by any means, electronic, mechanical, photocopying, recording or otherwise, without the prior written permission of the publisher.

Library of Congress Cataloging-in Publication
Condon, Anne, 1958-
   Legal lunacy/Anne Condon, Tom Condon
   p. cm.
   ISBN 0-8431-3404-6
   1. Law—United States—Humor. 2. Lawyers—United States—Humor
   3. Laws—United States—Popular works. I. Condon, Tom. II. Title.
   K184.C66 1992
   349.73 ' 00207—dc20
   [347.30207]   92-15940
                                                            CIP

NOTICE: The information contained in this book is true and complete to the best of our knowledge. All recommendations are made without any guarantees on the part of the author or of Price Stern Sloan, Inc. The author and publisher disclaim all liability in connection with the use of this information.

Dedication

To Clare and Jack

Acknowledgments

The cooperation, not to mention sense of humor, of many people contributed greatly to this book. We especially thank: Tom Lane, Eric Klein, Bill Carroll, J. Charles Mokriski, Deirdre Condon, Brian Dunigan, David Condon, Susan L. Anderson, Frank M. Masters, Al Bowright, Susan Savacki, Steve Cicilline, Betty Zeller, Susan E. Jaworowski, Kenneth C. Behringer, Virginia L. Brooks, John E. Smedberg, Michael R. Vanderburg, Andrew Kreig, Richard A. Cross, David Morse, Lori Grussmark, Constance Neyer, John Stieff, John Noliter, Scott Harrison, Paul Mount, John D. Olsrud, A. Peter Cannon, Tom Lukins, Earl McGinnes, Tamara Cook, Paul Jacques, Brian Zevnick, Michele Neves, Roy D. Bates, Dave Biklen, Kim Seckler, Bob Erickson, Ralph Eliot, Jim Fazzallaro, Jack Lavelle, Dennis Cooper and staff, Dan Wolcott, John McNeal, George Humphreys, Jeff Fleishman, Patti Peck, Jen DiSimone, Terry McKensie, Steve Collins, Norman Furse, Sam Keyes, Ray Puccinelli and Bernadette Dillon.

About the Authors

Tom Condon, a graduate of the University of Notre Dame and the University of Connecticut School of Law, is a newspaper columnist, television commentator and lawyer.

Anne Condon, a graduate of Boston University and former Associated Press reporter and editor, is a free-lance writer. They live in West Hartford, Conn., with their two children.

TABLE OF CONTENTS

Introduction

"No man's life or property is safe while the Legislature is in session."

—Mark Twain

In Woody Allen's movie *Bananas,* Woody, the alienated New Yorker, joins a band of revolutionaries in a banana republic. After much hardship they finally overthrow the ruling dictator. The rebel chief then becomes the new dictator, and immediately makes new laws—including one that all citizens must wear their underwear on the outside.

That may sound far-fetched, but it isn't.

We've collected loony legislation from federal, state and local lawmakers for "Legal Lunacy." Some are old, many are current, some are bills that are pending and others are proposals that never passed, but are humorous nonetheless. Our one regret is the laws we heard about but were unable to track down. In particular, we know a small town in Illinios banned electric "bug zappers" in 1991, but we couldn't find which town. Or why. Noise? Insects' rights movement? If you know about the bug zapper law, could you give us a call?

Tom and Anne Condon

Chapter

I

A Hunting Season for Attorneys and Other Gems of Politicians, by Politicians and Usually for Politicians

pettifogging shyster:

An unscrupulous (legal) practitioner who disgraces his profession by doing mean work and resorting to sharp practice to do it.

My Wild Irish Rose

There's never been much question that Chicago aldermen are powerful. One, the owner of a large flower shop, succeeded years ago in making it illegal for street vendors to sell flowers.

A Touchy Subject

No one is quite sure why it takes politicians 10 words to say what everyone else can say in one, but this has always been so. They insist on calling a spade a long-handled, single-bladed garden implement. In what may be a classic example of legislative wordiness, consider the anti-nudity ordinance under consideration in St. Augustine, Fla. County commissioners are mulling a law that contains a 328-word definition of "buttocks," and a 70-word definition of "breast." Here is part of the buttocks definition:

> "Buttocks: The area to the rear of the human
> body (sometimes referred to as the gluteus max-
> imus) which lies between two imaginary lines

running parallel to the ground when a person is standing, the first or top of such line being one-half inch below the top of the vertical cleavage of the nates (i.e., the prominance formed by the muscles running from the back of the hip to the back of the leg) and the second or bottom line being one-half inch above the lowest point of the curvature of the fleshy protuberance (sometimes referred to as the gluteal fold), and between two imaginary lines, one on each side of the body (the 'outside lines'), which outside lines are perpendicular to the ground and to the horizontal lines described above and which perpendicular outside lines pass through the outermost point(s) at which each nate meets the outer side of the leg...."

And it goes on from there. And on. As a local newspaper reporter said, they use 10 "ifs" and 11 "ands" to define "butts." The dictionary manages to define buttocks in two words: "the rump."

The ordinance is an effort to ban skimpy swimsuits from beaches and nude dancing in an establishment called "The Cafe Erotica." They could quite easily achieve their goals by making dancers and sunbathers wear copies of the ordinance.

Why Not Name It for Me?

There's no limit to the ego of most politicians. Take, for example, New Mexico legislator Tom Benavides. For years, Benavides has been trying to get the state to create a new county, named after, you guessed it, himself. His proposal almost passed when he finally relented and said the people who lived there could name it themselves.

Bad Way to Leave Office

Politics may be tough today, but things were tougher a few centuries ago, at least in New Mexico. In 1680, when the state was run by the Spanish, the Pueblo Indians rose in revolt. For the first and only time, the different tribes joined together, defeated the Spanish and scalped the colonial governor. The Indians ruled New Mexico for the next 12 years. But they proved that politicians everywhere have the same problems. The Indians started fighting among themselves, and the Spanish reconquered New Mexico. Thus ended "The Great Pueblo Revolt."

No Free Passes

The New Mexico Constitution prohibits railroads from giving free passes to politicians. It seems the railroads were very powerful at the time the constitution was written, and it was feared they would try to buy off the pols.

No Butts in the Booth

Just so no last-minute political deals are made in smoke-filled rooms, Kansas decided to do away with the smoke. An old law prohibits any candidate from handing out cigars on Election Day.

Desert Schooner

When Oklahoma organized its territorial legislature for its first 90-day session, much time was spent deciding where the state capital would be. In fact, the first 88 days were spent arguing over the location of the capital, leaving only two days for other business. Lawmakers rushed through a big bunch of bills that weren't too carefully reviewed. One of them empowered the territory to license sea pilots. Oklahoma is landlocked.

But Could Marx Play Football?

During the McCarthy era of the early 1950s, when there was a Commie in every corner, an Oklahoma legislator suggested that the University of Oklahoma's school color, red, was an indication communism was creeping into the school. The school weathered the storm and didn't change its colors. A Connecticut legislator of the same period decried fluoridization of drinking water as a "Communist plot."

Lanky Linen

Alfalfa Bill Murray was a legendary legislator in Oklahoma around the turn of the century who became speaker of the house and governor. He was also a tall fellow, and nothing ticked him off more than going into a hotel and having short sheets on the bed. In 1908 he had a law passed that required all hotels in the Sooner State to have sheets that covered the bed and had three extra feet of linen to cover the head and feet. The so-called "Nine Foot Sheet Law" stayed on the books for several decades, until after Alfalfa Bill went to his last resting place.

What's in a Name?

Supporters of laws often try to give them catchy names so the titles stick in the often vacant minds of legislators. And a name with a ring to it can be chanted at public hearings. Residents of Washington, D.C., came up with one a few years ago: "The Two and Blue in View" law. It was a request for more cops on foot patrols in the crime-plagued city. They chanted, "Two and Blue in View!" at hearings and meetings, but to no avail. The district didn't have the money, and the law didn't pass.

Went to the Big Sir

Georgia officials were revising their state laws in 1981, and noticed they still allowed pensions for Confederate widows. That week the last widow died. Lawmakers bowed their heads, and deleted the law.

Club Soda for All My Friends

In Washington state it's illegal for a candidate to buy anyone a drink on Election Day.

Why Did We Suspect This?

An old Virginia law was titled, "An Act to Prevent Corrupt Practices or Bribery by Any Person Other Than a Candidate."

Great Idea, But...

In 1985 an Arizona legislator proposed that each candidate for the legislature take a reading and an IQ test three months before the election. The scores would have been posted on the ballot, had the bill passed. But a majority of legislators, for whatever reason, voted it down.

Whose Brother-in-Law

In 1988 Indiana legislators cancelled an authorized monthly stipend for a fellow named Lester Bowles. The action was taken after an extensive survey indicated no one had any idea who Bowles was.

No Kidding

In Maryland two legislators named Masters and Johnson recently introduced a bill that would create a board to license sex therapists.

But It Was Satire

A 5-foot-5 legislator in Maryland, outraged by the popular satire "Short People" by singer-songwriter Randy Newman, several years ago introduced a bill to prohibit its playing by radio stations in the state. The attorney general short-circuited the attempt by ruling that such a law would be unconstitutional, declaring, "The First Amendment empowers musclemen to kick verbal sand in the faces of the short and the skinny, as well as Davids to aim hard words at towering Goliaths."

Weather Forecasting

A Utah legislator proposed a resolution urging that each TV weather person be required to provide an ice cream cone to every member of the state House of Representatives whenever the forecast was wrong. The resolution failed, perhaps on First Amendment grounds.

Answer That Thing

In California it's against regulations to let phones ring more than ten times in state offices.

Short People

An Arkansas legislator not long ago proposed that the state provide growth hormones to dwarfs.

Somehow Fitting

In Simsbury, Conn., it's illegal for a politician to campaign at the town dump.

By Hook or by Crook

If the Rushville, Ill., city council doesn't have a quorum, those present can have the cops go out and arrest absent members and drag them to the meeting.

Beam Me Up, Monsieur

We've tried to limit this book to American legislation, but we've been unable to find anything here like an ordinance passed in the 1950s by officials of Avignon, France, that made it illegal for any flying saucer to land in the city. As far as we know, all extraterrestrial aliens have observed the law to the letter.

Never Mind

A Maine legislator had an experience a few years ago that's happened to many of his colleagues. He introduced a bill to legalize hitchiking in the daytime. But the staff research wasn't quite what it should have been. Charles Webster had to withdraw his bill after learning that daytime hitchiking already was legal.

Utter Nonsense

A federal law makes it illegal to "utter" a false or counterfeit money order. Perhaps it's also illegal to mumble a phony $20 bill.

Call a Service

Each year, the mayor of Danville, Ky., must appoint "three intelligent housekeepers" to the Board of Tax Supervisors.

For Small Messes

An old federal law made it illegal to import tiny sponges, smaller than four inches in diameter.

Keep a Civil Tongue

Call a Vermont court a "kangaroo court" or some similar moniker, and you might be looking at a $200 fine. It is illegal to defame a court.

Power to the People

We often blame legislators—correctly—for writing loony laws and generally screwing things up. What if we gave the government back to the people, and let the people make laws directly? The Connecticut Department of Consumer Protection did something like this a few years ago. The department held a "There Ought to be a Law" contest, in which adults and children could submit proposals for new consumer laws. Some of our favorite entries included:

- A requirement that restaurants have nose-blowing sections and non-nose-blowing sections.

- A ban against potato chip bags and cereal boxes that are not full.

- A requirement that tea bags have a string that doesn't break.

- A law against "purloined and pilfered poultry parts," that is, a ban against chicken packagers putting extra gizzards, heads, necks and other junk parts into chickens to increase their weight.

- A ban against soda with no fizz.

- A requirement that all hamsters come with a guarantee.

- A law allowing patients to charge doctors who keep them waiting and customers to charge repairmen who never show up.

- A law that would make it illegal to say, "Have a nice day." The penalty would be increased if the speaker offered the pleasantry after delivering bad news.

- A ban on holiday sales that start more than two and a half weeks before the holiday.

- A requirement that department stores sell winter clothing in the winter and summer clothing in the summer.

- A rule that every law be easy to understand and be written in 50 words or less.

- A ban on anyone appearing on nude beaches except those who weigh less than 125 pounds.

- Heavy penalties against people who stop suddenly on escalator landings.

The contest brought in several more serious reponses as well, a few quite good. One has even been adopted. The consensus was the mix of the good, the bad and the silly was about the same as the legislature might have done.

Good Fence Laws Make Good Neighbors

Back when this was a more agricultural country, almost every town, county or state had "fence viewers," whose duty it was to settle disputes arising from fences. If the cattle from one farm broke through the fence and caused trouble on another farm, the fence viewers would be hauled out. Well, many officials, such as county commissioners in Kansas, are still fence viewers, and every once in a while they are called to settle a dispute—usually by an insurance company. In fact, the Kansas legislature was going to revise its fence laws not long ago because many farmers don't use fences anymore, but didn't because of pressure from the insurance companies. So they're left with fence laws such as the one that requires fence posts to be put near fence gates so people will have a place to tie their horses or teams while opening the gates.

Laws That Aren't Really Laws

Bogie never said, "Play it again, Sam," and Cary Grant never said, "Judy, Judy, Judy." But people think they did, and these legendary inaccuracies have become movie lore. So too with the law. All over the country there are laws people think are on the books, but they really aren't. These laws get reprinted in books and articles, discussed and perhaps even used in court. No one knows how it happens, but then no one knows how "Judy, Judy, Judy" got started, either. Here are some laws many people are convinced are real, but legal officials can't find on the books:

- Kansas is said to have a law that reads, "When two trains approach each other at a crossing, they shall both come to a full stop, and neither shall start up until the other has gone." It's a pity that isn't real.

- Key West, Fla., is said to ban turtle racing within the city limits. City officials say they get inquiries about the law from time to time, and always give people the same answer: There's no such law.

- Albuquerque, N.M., supposedly doesn't allow taxi drivers to reach out and pull passengers into their cabs. A big negative on that; neither city nor state lawyers can find hide nor hair of such a law. The state actually doesn't have many taxis. Maybe one driver hustling for business was ordered to cool his jets by some policeman.

- Hartford, Conn., is purported to prevent crossing the street on your hands. Such a stunt would doubtless stop traffic, but there's no law against it.

- Winston-Salem, N.C., has a phantom ordinance prohibiting anyone under the age of 7 from going to college. One wonders if this has caused any prodigies to matriculate in other states.

- New York supposedly had an older law that prohibited card-playing on trains. If that were true and it were still on the books, it would be the second-most violated law in the New York City area. The first has to be the city's anti-gridlock ordinance, a real law which orders drivers not to enter intersections unless they can get all the way through them. Hah.

- Idaho Falls, Idaho, is said to have a law prohibiting anyone over the age of 78 from riding a motorcycle. City officials say there's no such law, and who could blame them? If word got out, the Gray Panthers would come roaring through town on three-wheeled Harleys, smashing Geritol bottles and crashing the dance at the senior center. And who could blame them?

- Oklahoma supposedly passed a law making it illegal to catch a whale anywhere in the state. It's funny, what with the state having no coastline, but it just never happened.

- Kansas is said to have had a law, widely quoted, that restricted the length of a man's shirttails. Again, it isn't in any of the state's law books. Who knows? Maybe some tailor who was short of material came up with it one day and neglected to pursue legislative approval.

Tough Times

Bridgeport, Conn., has had a tough time with the law recently. The hard-pressed industrial city tried to file bankruptcy, only to find out it was against the law for a city to go bankrupt. Then a local legislator tried to introduce a bill in the Connecticut General Assembly that would dissolve the city and divide it up among its contiguous suburbs. That bill as yet hasn't passed. The residents are stuck with their town.

Just So We're Straight on This ...

The federal Employee Retirement Income Security Act defines an employee as "any individual employed by an employer."

Freudian Slip

Due to a typographical error, a routine ordinance in Shelbyville, Ind., about charging for bad checks started out: "Whereas, the city of Shelbyville through its various governmental facists receives numerous checks ..." This was changed to "governmental facets."

Gutter Language

Perhaps there's too much bureaucracy in this country. Redford Township, Mi., has a "Downspout Appeal Board."

Tax Those New Yorkers

An ordinance proposed in Robbins, N.C., states, "In the future, anyone not living within the immediate vicinity of Robbins must have a permit from the Chief of Police and okayed by the Mayor or one of the Commissioners." It's not clear what the permit is for, but they may be on to something.

Pac 'em In

North Carolina just passed a law saying a political action committee, or PAC, has to have a name that describes the group's cause or purpose. The idea is to prohibit, say, the highway or tobacco lobbies from calling themselves "Citizens for Good Government."

Ahem

Under a recent change in federal law, garment workers can now make mittens at home.

Civil War

Veterans of the Civil War constituted a powerful political force in this country for decades after the war, and if they wanted a law passed, it was usually passed. In Indiana, it was illegal to sell food within a half-mile of an old soldiers' picnic—until 1976.

Proper Burial

Federal mail fraud statutes prohibit misrepresenting the services offered by a pet cemetery.

Butt Squad

In a recent debate about smoke-free public buildings, one Arizona legislator suggested the state form an anti-smoking force, dressed in orange jumpsuits. The threat of an orange cop cruising into the restroom was too much even for ardent nonsmokers, and the weed force never materialized.

Aren't Some Things Private?

A Minnesota tax form is quite thorough. Some would say too thorough. It even asks for your date of death.

Here I Sit

Under the law of the state of Washington, any restroom with pay toilets has to have an equal number of free toilets. This law came to pass after the speaker of the state House of Representatives raced into an all-pay facility without a dime. We're told the man's bad luck continued. He was later indicted on racketeering charges, in an unrelated incident.

Chapter

II

No Puppets in the Window and Other Zany Laws from America's Big Cities and Small Towns

actuarius:

In Roman law, the officer who had charge of the public baths.

Ghoul Friend

It is illegal to loiter in the city morgue in Detroit.

No BVDs on BMWs

A regulation in San Francisco makes it unlawful to use used underwear to wipe off cars in a car wash.

It's All Garbage

Baltimore has regulations governing the disposal of hog's heads, pet droppings and oyster shells. Baltimore has so many ordinances related to trash that a local politician offered the following observation: "If the Eskimos have 32 words for snow because it's central to their lives, trash must be central to the lives of the residents of Baltimore."

Move with Care

In Baltimore it's illegal to block the sidewalk with a box. But the offense only carries a $1 fine. Another law makes it illegal to throw a bale of hay (or of anything else) out a second-story window. That gets you a $20 fine. If the bale happens to land on a passerby, you have an additional problem.

Especially Near the Subways

To cut down on its once-horrific graffiti problem, New York City several years ago made it illegal to carry an open can of spray paint. City officials say the law actually did cut down on the amount of Gotham graffiti.

Peace and Quiet

Noise ordinances are making a comeback around the country, spurred on by people who want to get some sleep. In Berkeley, Calif., you can't whistle for an escaped bird before 7 A.M. In San Antonio, Texas, you can't honk a horn, run a generator, have a revival meeting or do anything else that disturbs the neighborhood —and the city has a four-member noise police squad to enforce the law.

It's Too Dark

In North Carolina it's illegal to sell cotton lint at night. It's also illegal to sell cotton seed at night. We were in Raleigh recently, and we can report that it's still legal to buy cotton shorts during the day.

The Iceman Goneth

It's still the law in North Chicago, Ill., that anyone who wants to deliver ice has to pay a $25 fee and have an accurate scale on his vehicle. Enforcement has been easy since this new-fangled electronic refrigeration caught on.

Councilman Scrooge

A city council member in Albuquerque, N.M., introduced a resolution a few years ago to ban Santa Claus from the city. The spirit of Christmas prevailed, and the matter was defeated.

Melancholy Baby

If you've got a gal in Kalamazoo, better whisper sweet nothings to her. An old law forbade swains from serenading their sweeties from outside the window.

Not Until After Brunch

It's illegal in New York to start any kind of public performance, show, play, game or what have you, until after 1:05 P.M. This may explain why the Giants moved to New Jersey.

Makes Perfect Sense

In New York it's unlawful for any person to do any thing that is against the law. Lest there be any confusion.

Do a Figure Eight

New York drivers are known to be crazy, but so are pedestrians in the Empire State. The law may be part of the problem. Jaywalking is legal, as long as it's not diagonal. That is, you can cross the street out of the crosswalk, but you can't cross a street diagonally. It may be helpful to mention this to some guy who is trying to wash your windshield in midtown Manhattan. Then again, it may not.

After Midnight

A Boston mayor who disliked dancing and liked to retire early once banned midnight dancing in the Hub City.

That's a Relief

In Boston it's illegal to post an advertisement on a public urinal. It's also against the law to hang a vending machine on a utility pole.

Kind Word and a Gun

Under an 1872 law still on the books, an alderman in Chicago can carry a gun. Frighteningly, some do.

The Hooker Hook

A "john" who patronizes a prostitute in Portland, Ore., risks having his car towed and impounded. City officials say this new law has cut down on repeat offenders, presumably who have had to explain the problem to their wives.

Safe Streets

In Hartford, Conn., it's illegal to plant a tree in the street. In Boston it's illegal to cut firewood in the street, or shoot a bow and arrow in the street. In New York City it's illegal to throw swill into the street. In Forest City, N.C., it's against the law to shoot dice in the street.

It Better Not Be Memorex

San Francisco bans any "mechanical device that reproduces obscene language."

Bless You

San Francisco prohibits kerchoo powders and stink balls.

Such a Deal

New Yorkers must feel guilty about taking Manhattan from the Indians for $24. Members of nine New York Indian tribes are exempt from the city's 8 percent parking tax—but the law doesn't help them find a space.

No Can Do

In a law that predates returnable bottles and cans, it's illegal in Boston to rummage through rubbish containers.

Clean Streets

In Danville, Ky., it's illegal to throw slops or soapsuds in the street.

Punch and Judy

New York City may be the theater capital of the country, but it's illegal to have a puppet show in your window and a violation can land you in the snoozer for 30 days.

What About Sling Shots?

In Forest City, N.C., it's illegal to bring a pea shooter to a parade. It's also illegal to shoot paper clips with rubber bands.

Jo, Not Yo

Take some elocution lessons if you're going to Joliet, Ill., where it's against the law to mispronounce the city's name. Offenders can be fined up to $500.

Just Look

In Salem, Oregon, it's illegal for patrons of establishments that feature nude dancing to be within two feet of the dancers.

Tan Your Hide

New York now has inspectors who check tanning parlors.

Short People

"Dwarf-tossing," the strange practice of hurling dwarfs in padded suits, is outlawed in the bars of Springfield, Ill., because it's dangerous and exploitative. Curiously, the practice is apparently allowed elsewhere in town, with a special permit.

But Wait

In Christiansburg, Va., it's illegal to "spit, expectorate or deposit any sputum, saliva or any form of saliva or sputum."

A Tree Is a Tree

Oakland, Calif., makes it illegal to grow a tree in front of your neighbor's window and block his view. However, you're off the hook if the tree is one that town officials consider an attractive tree, such as a redwood or box elder.

Say What?

In Oxford, Miss., it's illegal to "create unnecessary noises."

They Just Fly Away

Balloons with advertising on them are illegal in Hartford, Conn.

No Early Rays

In Provincetown, Mass., it's illegal to sell suntan oil until after noon on Sunday.

Don't Step in It

In Boston it's against the law to keep manure in a building unless the building is being used as a stable. If it is, you can keep up to two cords of manure. If you're overstocked, you need a permit to remove the stuff. And you can't leave it in the street.

Tip of the Hat

It wasn't actually a law, but by gentlemen's agreement no one in Philadelphia was supposed to build a building higher than the top of William Penn's hat. The hat was part of the statue of the city's founder that stands on the roof of city hall. The agreement held until the mid-1980s.

God Bless 'em

Perhaps anticipating telemarketing, the town fathers of Albany, Ga., have for years prohibited peddlers from using the telephone to either sell things or raise funds.

Karl Who?

The Evil Empire is falling apart, and the folks of Haines City, Fla., can pat themselves on the back. They've outlawed Communism since 1950.

Be Gone

Under an 1889 law, the health officer of East Jordan, Mich., could send any nonresident with an infectious disease back to where he came from, as long as the person could travel. If not, the officer could rent a house for use as a pest house.

Hotfoot Law

In the hippy-dippy late 60s, Youngstown, Ohio, briefly had a law making it illegal to walk barefoot through town.

Keep It in Your Pocket

The people in Manteno, Ill., do not want used facial tissue, period. Hence, you cannot "throw, drop or place" a used hankie "upon any public way or public place or upon the floor of any convenience or upon the floor of any theater, hall or assembly or public building or upon the surface or any lot or parcel of ground or on the roof on any building or in any light or air shaft, court or areaway."

Keep the Pants On

In Minoola, Ill., it's illegal to take your clothes off and "expose the naked person" during daylight or twilight, even if all you're doing is taking a bath.

Unfortunate Term

By town law the sewer service charge in Belhaven, N.C., used to be "$2 per month, per stool." It was recently changed to read "per toilet."

Short on Plot

Funeral jargon seems to have crept into the wording of a cemetery fee regulation in Norton, Ohio. There regular plots are $33, but "creamies" are $75.

Nocturnal Solitude

The good people of Tryon, N.C., are serious about getting a good night's sleep. It's against the law for anyone to keep "fowl that shall cackle," or for anyone to play the piccolo between the hours of 11 P.M. and 7:30 A.M.

Department of Redundancy Department

In Dana, Ind., the town seal has the words "TOWN SEAL" right in the middle.

No Clip Joints

As in many towns, you need a permit to run a barbershop in Christiansburg, Va. But the wording of the town's law indicates that the permit will be revoked if you're caught operating without a permit.

Long Toot of the Law

In Christiansburg, Va., it's illegal to imitate a police whistle.

I See Trouble Ahead

Gypsies should stear clear of Caroline County, Md., where, I predict, it's a $100 fine or six months in the can for "forecasting or pretending to foretell the future."

As It Should Be

In Xenia, Ohio, it's illegal to spit in a salad bar.

Stranger, Hop the Train

Strangers in Simsbury, Conn., were required, under an ordinance enacted in 1701 and only recently repealed, to leave town within a month unless they had at least 20 shillings to their names.

Wait for the Light

Under an old law in Marblehead, Mass., it was illegal to cross the street on Sunday, unless absolutely necessary.

Life's a Dream

It sounds like the title of a rock album or something, but "Coasting on Beaver Street" is illegal in Edgeworth, Pa.

Black Is Black

In Robbins, N.C., anyone who refuses to black out after hearing the blackout signal is subject to a $5 fine.

Size Is Relative

An ordinance in Murray, Ky., says the superintendent of sanitation "shall determine whether a person is small, medium or large." Why the superintendent should make this determination is left unsaid.

Watch It

By law, "watch stuffers" are unwelcome in McKeesport, Pa. Now, no one is quite sure what a watch stuffer does, but whatever he does, he better do it somewhere else.

Oh Yeah?

It used to be against the law in Jonesboro, Ga., to utter the words, "Oh boy."

Josef Who?

Miami Shores Village, Fla., has for years required that all goods made in Communist countries and offered for sale in Miami Shores Village be clearly marked as such. The ordinance notes that such goods are often marked in a "false, misleading or inadequate manner, to hide their Communist origins."

Watch the Fine Print

In Rockwell, N.C., anyone who violates the terms of a proclamation—such as failing to appropriately celebrate Peanut Day or Jaycees Week—is guilty of a misdemeanor.

What About Art?

A 1950 anti-obscenity law in Irondale, Ala., prohibited any showing of anyone nude or "in a substantially nude state" except a babe in arms.

Sling It

David would have been in trouble if he'd challenged Goliath in Jonesboro, Tenn., where a slingshot used to be classified by law as a deadly weapon.

Of Sheets and Shirts

Many jurisdictions have laws requiring hotels and inns to provide such things as clean linens, bug-free pillows and screens on windows. Innkeepers in Salem, Mass., however, used to be required to provide guests with clean nightshirts.

Chapter

III

You Used to Be Able to Punish Your Teenager— The Wishful Laws We've Made About Children

boy:

In early common law, the word meant "legitimate child."

But I Was Really Sick

Truancy was no laughing matter in turn-of-the-century Boston. Skipping one day of school without a good reason could land a boy in reform school for two years. Needless to say, the situation has changed.

Honest, Mister, It's My Mother's Ring

In Fort Wayne, Ind., it's illegal to let your children sell your jewelry.

Father, Come Home From the Bar

In Indiana you can't drink beer with a child present in the room.

They Ain't Fagin

In Rappahannock, Va., adults who don't work, but instead hire out their minor children and live off their wages, are considered vagrants.

No Kidding

A Washington state law offers the presumption that youngsters will read comic books.

Gone but Not Forgotten

If you think kids have it easy today, you're right. Under the Code of 1650 in the New Haven Colony (in what is now Connecticut), a 16-year-old boy could be put to death if he "cursed, struck or disobeyed" his parents or was "stubborn or rebellious."

The Wrong Track

Wisconsin law provides for a fine of $2 to $20 for anyone under age 17 caught jumping onto a railroad car while the train is in motion.

Good Luck

In a case of wishful thinking, a Delaware legislator recently proposed a law that would require every minor to inform his or her parents before engaging in sexual intercourse.

Good Luck II

It used to be the law in Hawaii that children had to obey all "lawful and moral" commands of their parents.

'T' for Trouble

Video parlors be damned, the folks of Olympia, Wash., know that trouble starts with "t" and that rhymes with "p" and that stands for pool. Minors are prohibited from frequenting pool halls.

Spiderman Made Me Do It

In Washington state it's illegal to sell to minors comics that might incite them to violence or depraved or immoral acts. Of course, they can always watch television.

Cher and Cher Alike

A Wisconsin legislator recently introduced a bill making it illegal to tattoo someone under the age of 18. The solon was quoted as saying, "I'm going to save the buttocks of a few juveniles."

The Cutting Edge

In Mesquite, Texas, it's still against regulations for youngsters to have haircuts that are "startling or unusual."

But I'm Howard Hughes, Jr.

In Washington it's illegal to pretend you're the child of a rich person and entitled to his estate.

Haute Couture

Wyoming required that every inmate of the state's training school for girls be issued crinoline bloomers.

What a Money Maker

Under a 1959 ordinance, stubborn children were considered vagrants in Jupiter Inlet Colony, Fla.

Chapter
IV

No Sleeping in the Outhouse and Other Laws About Property

droit d'aubaine:

Under this old rule, if you died while traveling in France, the government could take your luggage, your money and anything else you owned and keep it. The rule was abolished in 1819.

When There Were Buffalo in Buffalo

In colonial New York, it was illegal to buy land from the Indians without a license.

There Goes the Neighborhood

It is illegal to move a building in Minooka, Ill., without a permit and the written permission of a majority of the owners of the property within a 200-foot radius of the lot to where the building is to be moved.

Abe Lincoln, Call Your Office

In Maine, buildings made of round logs are tax exempt.

Where Else Do You Keep Them?

An old law in Scottsbluff, Neb., prohibited the storing of snowballs in a refrigerator.

It Makes a Nice Tea

In North Carolina it's illegal to dig ginseng on other people's property between the months of April and September, according to an 1866 law.

How About a Water Bed?

If you happen to own a marl bed in North Carolina, the law demands that you put a fence around it. A marl bed may not be what you think. It is a kind of rock quarry.

No Comment

Apparently with an exaggerated idea of the laws of thermal dynamics, the city council of West Palm Beach, Fla., once decreed that the roofs of all outhouses be fireproof.

And Fall in the Hall

In Los Angeles years ago it was legal to cook in your bedroom, but not to sleep in your kitchen.

Prone to Trouble

An old law in Columbus, Ga., made it illegal to sit on your porch in an indecent position.

Ship of Fuels

New Jersey just passed a law saying the cap on the oil fill spout that leads into the oil storage tank in your basement either has to be green or have the words "fuel oil" written on it. "Why?" you might ask. It seems the state had several unfortunate incidents where heating oil delivery trucks went to the wrong homes. The home-owners had had their oil tanks removed, but still had old fill spouts on the outside of the dwellings. The deliverymen pumped hundreds of gallons of oil into their basements.

Beats Me

In San Francisco it's illegal to beat a rug in front of your house.

Damn Yankees

If the South rises again, Kennesaw, Ga., will be ready. The town makes it illegal for every homeowner *not* to own a gun, unless you are a convicted felon, conscientious objector or disabled.

Son of a Gun

In Ballwin, Mo., the only place you can use vulgar, obscene or indecent language is in your home.

Don't Look Down

In Washington state it's illegal to sleep in an outhouse without the owner's permission.

Who Would Notice?

In New York City it's illegal to shake a dust mop out a window.

Go Ahead

In Colorado it's now legal to remove the furniture tags that say, "Do Not Remove Under Penalty of Law."

Sleep on It

In Washington state, until quite recently, you could have been fined up to $500 for removing or defacing the label on a pillow.

Use Orange Crates

Because people were using them for cheap furniture, it's now illegal in North Carolina to take and sell labeled milk crates.

Taxing Event

Taxpayers of Bainbridge, Ind., used to have to swear a solemn oath that the values they placed on their taxable property were the fair market values.

Chain of Events

In colonial times, Hartford, Conn., had an ordinance that allowed any resident to rent the town chain for 2 pence. The resident had to fix it if he broke it.

Even a Two-Holer

In Danville, Ky., its illegal to enter another person's outhouse without his permission.

Hot Horsemeat

In Washington state it's illegal to have horsemeat in the house if it's for your dog.

Boom!

Between January 15 and June 15, it's illegal to blast within 1,500 feet of a commercial hatchery or fur farm in the state of Washington without giving the owner a warning 24 hours in advance. It's not clear what the owner can do in the intervening 24 hours. Perhaps pass out ear plugs?

Where Bossie Is Boss

Most agricultural states bend over backwards to protect farmers. For example, theft of a cow, colt or mule can land you in jail for seven years in Kansas. Crimes such as theft of diamonds, blackmail or extortion carry lesser sentences.

Chapter

V

No Fake Wrestling and Other Laws About Sports

baseball:

The national pastime was once held in violation of Pennsylvania's Sunday closing laws because "when played by professionals for profit, it is a performance of worldy employment and business."

pg. 41

Pointed Controversy

Illinois just passed a "Balloon Dart Game Permit Act," which regulates how much air must be in balloons in dart games at county fairs. It seems some darts were bouncing off underinflated balloons. Rather than demand sharper darts, or encourage patrons to throw harder, legislators ordered more air into the balloons. Next they'll want softballs that actually fit into those milk bottles. Or basketballs that fit through those small rims. Or footballs that fit through those Volkswagen tires. Or …

My Second Will Handle the Details

It's against the law in Arizona to fight a duel. It's also a violation if you know about a dueling challenge and don't report it…even if the challenge hasn't yet been sent!

No Booze for Yoooz

In Hawaii it's illegal for a shooting gallery to offer liquor as a prize. The shooter might want to come back after drinking the prize and try again.

Day of Rest

In Baltimore it's illegal to play professional croquet before 2 P.M. on Sunday. The law also applies to professional quoits.

Know When to Fold 'em

Both Massachusetts and New Hampshire had old laws that penalized gamblers who lost money. You'd get fined in Massachusetts if you had any money left. In New Hampshire you were prohibited from pawning the clothes off your back to pay off gambling debts.

The Compleat Angle

In the state of Washington it's illegal to catch a fish by throwing a rock at it (and this includes rock bass). It's also against the law to molest food fish or shellfish. For all of this, one of the easiest ways for a fisherman to cheat is legal: You can discharge an explosive device in the water, if you can get a permit.

Don't Bet on It

Vermont's old gambling law encouraged folks to gamble at home. If you were caught, it was a $5 fine. But if you were caught gambling in a gaming house, the fine went up to $200. And if the gaming house had gaming equipment in it, add another $200. And if the house took a cut, another $200. Finally, you could incur an additional fine if you won money and, to add insult to injury, if you lost money. But times change. The state now has a lottery, and recently repealed its law banning the practice of betting on elections.

Dueling Bozos

An old Ohio law made it illegal for anyone who'd been caught dueling to hold public office.

Run a Mile for a Camel

In recent years, several efforts have been made to legalize camel racing and ostrich racing in New Mexico, but to no avail. Those bills were defeated, but the legislature recently allowed gambling on bicycle races. No one as yet has opened a parimutuel velodrome, we're told.

Railbirds' Holiday

Delaware prohibits horse racing of any kind on Good Friday and Easter Sunday.

Spare Me

Under Delaware law, any person of good moral character may keep and operate a bowling alley. No gambling, however, is allowed. And the alley must be kept in an orderly fashion, meaning, we suppose, no cigarette butts or empty beer cans on the scoring table.

Don't Tell the Cincinnati Kid

Riverboat gamblers in Iowa have a $5 maximum bet.

Take the Points

In Las Vegas you can bet on any team—except The University of Nevada at Las Vegas.

Small Clams Court

It's illegal to clam at night in Connecticut.

C'mon Seven

Due to a typographical error in the Tempe, Ariz., code, a shooting range can be run by the "Amateur Crapshooting Association."

They Don't Shoot Horses

The state of Washington doesn't allow marathon dancing—or marathon skipping, sliding, gliding, rolling or crawling.

Wrong, Whatever It Is

San Francisco has an ordinance prohibiting "cane games." City officials have no idea what cane games are. But when revising city laws recently, officials decided to keep the prohibition on the books, in case someday, somehow, cane games came back, they were deemed improper and the city needed the law.

Say It Ain't So, Hulk

Washington state doesn't allow fake wrestling.

Geronimo!

In Maryland the Legislature once proposed a board of parachute examiners to be made up of five licensed parachute instructors who would test and license all other parachute instructors. The plan had to be abandoned when it was learned there were only three licensed parachute instructors in the state.

Hold 'em, Fold 'em

In North Dakota, charitable groups can hold stud poker games to raise money, but only twice a year.

Five Card Draw

In San Francisco it's illegal to play poker in public or gamble in a barricaded room.

Just As Well

In Maine it's illegal to catch lobsters with your bare hands. The lobsters are under no similar constraints.

Sign Here, Kid

In Indiana a sports agent is supposed to give a college ten days' notice before luring a star athlete into the professional ranks.

It Scares the Horse

In Idaho it's illegal to hunt from the back of an animal. In Iowa it's illegal to hunt from an aircraft.

Yo, Bullwinkle

It's a crime in Alaska to hunt "anterless moose" unless a special season has been declared. If that's the case, stay away from the Moose Lodge. It's also against the law in Fairbanks to give a moose a beer.

Whatever It Is

The game of crackaloo is illegal in Fairfield, Ala.

Clean Slate

In Mooresville, N.C., it's illegal to attach anything to a pool table.

No Problem

It's illegal to clean salmon along Maine's upper Kennebec River. Enforcement of this law has been made easier for many years by the fact that, because of a dam, there are no salmon on the upper Kennebec River.

My Second Will Serve the Sentences

An old Washington law sent duelists to jail for ten years, assuming they didn't lose the duel.

Gone but Not Forgotten

The New York State Senate passed a resolution to commemorate the 25th anniversary of the Brooklyn Dodgers' 1955 world championship and expressed a longing that someday the Dodgers will return to "their one and only true home."

Sue the Ref!

A proposed Washington law protects sports referees from civil suit unless their actions were "willful, wanton, reckless, malicious or grossly negligent."

Hey, Ref, You're Blind

Punching an official at a youth sports program in Nashville, N.C., incurs a three-year suspension from the program for adult specators as well as participants.

Chapter
VI

Separation of Church and Snake—Supernatural Laws About Religion, God and Man

act of elizabeth:

The law of Elizabeth I which makes the King or Queen "the only supreme head on earth of the Church of England having full power to correct all errors, heresies, abuses, offenses, contempts and enormities."

Who Do? Me Do?

A minister in Pennsylvania is not supposed to perform a marriage ceremony if either the bride or the groom is drunk.

Be Gone, Serpent

In Kentucky, according to an old law, it's illegal to use any kind of reptile in a religious service. It's not certain if the law would withstand First Amendment scrutiny today.

You Can't Fool God

If you went to church in Texas years back, you'd better be recognized. An old law made it illegal to go to church in disguise.

I Swear to God I'm an Atheist

It used to be a $200 fine in Vermont to deny the "existence or being of God." Perhaps you could get off with a warning if you said you weren't sure.

If It's a Chicken Ranch, It Better Have Chickens

It's illegal in Nevada to have a "house of ill fame" within 400 yards of a church or school.

Elmer Gantry, Call Your Office

A recent proposal that ministers walk the beat with police officers in Belmont, N.C., notes "the ministers will carry a Bible instead of a gun."

Unholy Water

It's against a Key West, Fla., ordinance to spit on a church floor.

Who's Got the Button?

Idaho and other states allow members of the Native American Church to use the hallucinogenic plant peyote in religious services.

Wear Dark Glasses

It's unlawful to attract a crowd in Forest City, N.C., except when preaching the Gospel, politicking or "serenading on occasion of public rejoicing."

Pray for No. 3

In Spokane, Wash., it used to be illegal to interrupt a religious meeting by having a horse race.

Church and State?

The Delaware Constitution regulates bingo games.

Chapter
VII

Eat, Drink and Get Arrested—
Laws About Food and Drink

boston cream pie:

A Washington, D.C. court has held that the legal definition of this dessert is "two layers of sponge cake with a layer of a sort of cream custard."

What a Pickle

A century ago, cities all over the country enacted "pickle laws," for one reason or another. The most famous is doubtless the "Trenton Pickle Ordinance" in Trenton, N.J., made famous by writer Dick Hyman in books and articles. This law made it illegal to throw tainted pickles into the street. A Rhode Island town, Central Falls, made it illegal to throw pickle juice on trolley tracks. Connecticut made it illegal to sell pickles that collapsed and fell apart when dropped from a height of 12 inches. The pickle must "remain whole and even bounce," the law said. Boston's pickle law went a step further, and said a pickle should bounce four inches when dropped from waist height. Los Angeles made it illegal to make pickles anywhere in town, for fear the odor would offend, if anyone could detect it through the smog.

It Went Over Hard

A new health regulation in New Jersey bans the serving of eggs over easy, or any other kind of runny eggs. State officials were worried about salmonella. But the rule prompted so much national hilarity—comedian Johnny Carson asked why the state was worried about runny eggs when it was possible to buy machine guns there—that the governor decided to reconsider the matter. The "egg reg" is now on the back burner.

A Roll Is a Roll

In Washington state, where breadstuff is important stuff, it's illegal to make Parker House rolls unless you used enriched white flour, 100 percent wheat flour or graham flour.

When Honey Gets Blue

If the honey you are eating in Seattle is a blend of honey from two or more types of flowers, it's illegal for the honey to be labeled as having come from one type of flower. So if that's the case, stop eating it and get rid of it. Flush it, if you must. Possession of unlawful honey is—unlawful.

Cut Him Off

It's not clear what this has done to the bar business, but a law in North Chicago, Ill., makes it illegal to serve liquor to the feeble-minded.

But Begging Is OK

It's against the law in Vermont for vagrants to procure food by force. Apparently if you have a good job and stable home life, it's OK to procure food by force.

This Town Is Dry, Bud

In Mississippi it's illegal to buy beer in a "wet" town and then drive it through a "dry" town, even if you are trying to drive to your own home.

Unhand That Crawdaddy

That the folks in Louisianna take their food seriously is beyond question. It is against state law to steal even a single crawfish.

No Pie in the Face

If you've ever been to Mardi Gras in New Orleans, you'll see the kings and queens on the various floats throwing plastic money, medallions and jewels to the crowd, but not food. It's against the law to throw food from a float in the Mardi Gras festivities.

Know When to Say When

It's legal to walk down the street with a drink in New Orleans, even to drive with a drink. But if you fall over and block the sidewalk, you've just broken the law.

Lifesaver Yes, Wafer No

In one of the strangest Sunday laws we've come across, it used to be legal in Minnesota to sell rolled candy on Sunday, and illegal to sell flat candy. The wafer people have gotten this one repealed.

Butter, Butter, Butter, Butter

As in most dairy states, Vermont does what it can to discourage the use of margarine. For example, it's illegal to use colored margarine in restaurants unless the menu indicates you do—in letters two inches high. Colored margarine can only be served in triangle-shaped patties.

It's Still Good for Weddings

Georgia has 75 laws on how to build rice paddies, even though the state has only one rice farm left. Rice was the state's No. 1 crop before the Civil War. But right after the war, a hurricane destroyed all the paddies and ponds. It was too expensive to replace them without slaves, so the Rice State began growing peaches, peanuts and other crops. Georgia, by the way, has one of our favorite commissions, the Peanut Commission, which promotes peanut marketing and research.

Use Sen-Sen

It used to be against the law to go to the theater in Gary, Ind., after eating garlic.

Don't Spare the Tonic

An old law in Waterloo, Neb., discouraged barbers from eating onions on the job.

Get It to Go

You may deserve a break today, but you won't get it in Bloomfield, Conn., if you can't wait to get home from your local fast food emporium: It's against the law to eat in your car.

Cold Hands, Warm Heart

It's illegal to carry an ice cream cone in your pocket in Lexington, Ky.

Legislated Vegetable

Tomatoes are actually a fruit, but legally speaking, they're a vegetable. Ruling in an 1893 tariff case, the U.S. Supreme Court said that because tomatoes are normally eaten during a meal and not afterward, they are legally vegetables.

On the Rocks

One of the early Occupational Safety and Health Act laws in effect prohibited the use of ice in drinking water. It's been repealed.

And the Gravy?

The Iowa Legislature once passed a resolution ordering the state cafeteria to start serving cornbread.

Say, 'Cheese'

In Wisconsin you need a cheesemaker's license to make any kind of cheese, except Limburger. To make Limburger, you need a master cheesemaker's license.

Old Red Eye

Many states have had whacky liquor regulations. In Nevada until the 1960s it was illegal to sell liquor:

- at religious camp meetings;

- within a half-mile of the state prison;

- in the State Capitol Building;

- to imbeciles.

Also, saloon keepers had to post the names of habitual drunkards if so requested by the local sheriff or members of the imbibers' immediate families.

I'm Fine, Occifer

It used to be illegal to get drunk in Miami Beach, Fla., but the law has been repealed.

Two Fuzzy Navels, Please

California just legalized the sale of alcoholic beverages in nudist colonies.

Sweet Revenge

Minnesota has repealed its so-called "Twinkie" law, under which a Minneapolis City Council candidate was indicted for dispensing $34 worth of Twinkies®, Ho-Ho®s, cookies, Kool-Aid® and coffee to some senior citizens.

Good News for the Civilized World

Montana just legalized the production of caviar.

Big Bubble

In New York City you need a permit to transport carbonated beverages.

Did the Town Go for Carter?

In Mooresville, N.C., it's illegal to throw peanut hulls on the floor of town hall.

On St. Patrick's Day?

Magnolia, Ark., regulates the sale of green meats.

Think Nutrition

A North Dakota law used to provide for a penalty of up to 90 days in jail and a $1,000 fine for anyone convicted of making, selling or possessing candy cigarettes.

Domestic Is Different

In Washington you need a state license to be a wild mushroom dealer.

Oleo, My Oleo

It used to be illegal to "make, transport, handle, possess, sell, serve or use" yellow oleomargarine in Washington state. But the law said it was legal to eat it in private homes.

Pratfall Penalty

Funny or not, it's illegal to throw a banana peel on the sidewalk in Tennessee.

It's Just a Feather in My Cap

Anyone in Washington state who operates a macaroni factory has to file a sworn statement with the director of agriculture giving the prices to be charged for each type of macaroni to be made.

A Far, Far Butter Thing I Do

In North Dakota it's illegal to advertise buttered popcorn unless the popcorn has butter on it.

Washington Slept It Off Here

It is illegal in Michigan to use pictures of deceased ex-presidents to sell alcoholic beverages.

Watch on the Rind

According to a 1920 law, it was illegal to eat watermelon on the sidewalks or curbs of Mayfield, Ky., except for the east side of Court Square, where barrels were set up for rinds.

Wet Isn't Enough

You can get up to six months in jail in Vermont for selling fake mineral water. It is unclear if someone takes water down to the assay office to see if its minerals are real or fake, but that's the law.

No Goobers

In New Mexico products advertised as containing pinyon nuts actually have to contain pinyon nuts.

Chapter

VIII

You Can Only Marry an Old Cousin— Laws About Sex and Marriage

ubi nullum matrimonium, ibi nulla dos:

Where there is no marriage, there is no dowry.

Kissin', Wheezin' Cousins

Under Arizona law, first cousins can marry if they are both over the age of 65. If one cousin is under 65 they can still tie the knot, the law says, if proof that they cannot reproduce has been presented to a superior court judge.

We're Just Good Friends

It's still against the law in Arizona—and a Class 3 misdemeanor—for a person to live in "open and notorious cohabitation."

Wolf At Bay

An old law in Abilene, Texas, makes it illegal to whistle at girls. This may seem quaint, but complaints by feminists of harassment of women walking by building sites by male construction workers has brought calls for new laws not too different from the old ones.

Patently Absurd

Oxford and Cleveland, Ohio, and other cities (and many Catholic schools!) once had rules against women wearing patent leather shoes. The theory was that some overly curious, spurious member of the opposite sex would use the shiny surface as a mirror to sneak a peek. These laws do seem quaint, when compared to today's MTV standards.

Knit One, Hang Two

In the town of Mexico, Mo., it's illegal for women to knit while serving on juries.

Sexist Sow

North Carolina has a rarity, a sexist law that discriminates against men. It's the state's tramp law. Anyone convicted of being a tramp—one who goes from one place to another begging—can be fined $50, which he probably doesn't have, or popped in the snoozer for 30 days. But the law only applies to adult males. The Tarheel state more than makes up for that one with laws favoring men, such as a 19th century law that allows a husband to sign a deed for the couple but doesn't offer a wife the same right.

In North Carolina it's illegal to speak to a woman attending a college for women while on school property.

Just a Champagne Cocktail

In Manteno, Ill., it's against the law to allow a woman in a bar if the woman is trying to get men to buy her drinks. A waitress, can, however, still take drink orders.

The Second Time Around

For years it was illegal in Vermont for a divorced couple to move back in and live together again. The state apparently felt that if it went through the trouble of dissolving the marriage, it wasn't going to stand by and let its undoing be undone.

The Good Old Days

A Vermont law, repealed a few years ago, made it illegal to post an advertisement for a cure for "lost manhood, sexual weakness, lost vitality, impotency, gleet" and other maladies in any public place, including an outhouse.

At the No-Tell Motel

Vermont recently repealed its well known "persons found in bed together" law. A man found in bed with another's wife, or a woman found in bed with another's husband, "under circumstances affording the presumption of illicit intention" could formerly be tossed in jail for three years.

Next to the Bible

A few years ago a New Mexico legislator proposed putting free condoms in every hotel room in the state. The measure was defeated.

Don't Try It Now

Centuries ago, before equal rights and feminism, men made laws and women had to live with them. Women were prohibited from doing everything from wrestling and parachuting to wearing shorts and men's pants. Women were prohibited from flirting in some towns, and riding in a car with a man in others. In Minnesota women were supposed to "dress like women," and a woman was not allowed to imitate Santa Claus. In Arkansas it was legal for a man to beat his wife, as long as he did it no more than once a month. In Alabama a man could chastise his wife "with a stick no larger than your thumb."

What God Has Joined Together

Oklahoma lawmakers were worried about the high divorce rate a few years ago and were determined to do something about it. State Rep. Linda Larason advanced an amendment saying at the time of marriage, before receiving a license, both parties should agree:

• That neither party shall snore;

• No pantyhose shall be left hanging on the shower rod;

• Household responsibilities shall be shared equally;

• Each party shall be required to shut off the TV and put aside reading material or other handiwork while the other party is speaking;

• At least one meal a week shall be eaten out or prepared by the non-primary cook;

• Toothpaste shall be squeezed only from the bottom of the tube and caps shall always be replaced;

• The toilet seat shall always be left in the down position, except during use.

A male legislator debated the toilet seat position, but to no avail. The stardards were found impossibly high, and the measure defeated.

How About a Chastity Belt?

Several years ago, Oklahoma legislators were debating a bill to "asexualize sex offenders." The proposal went down to defeat for two reasons. The lawmakers figured they couldn't apply the law only to men, and the mostly male legislature couldn't figure out how to "asexualize" women, whatever that meant.

For Love and Money

In the early 1970s, during a tax debate, a Rhode Island legislator proposed a state tax on sex. This occassioned an uproar of jokes and editorial cartoons of assessors sitting on branches outside windows, etc. However, the speaker of the House of Representatives was not amused, and ordered the bill withdrawn. It was the first time in memory a bill was so defeated. Nonetheless, sex keeps working its way into legislative proposals. In a debate not long ago on a palimony bill in Oklahoma, a legislator proposed that both parties sign consent forms in triplicate before having sex. This proposal also went down to defeat.

Looking for Mr. Badbar

If you sign up for a dating service in Illinois, the state is there to protect you. The service has to give you a written contract, and you have three days in which to cancel (in case you get lucky that night on your own). They allow no financing on membership fees for more than three years. And here's the real advantage of the law: If you die, you're only liable for the charges up to the time of your death.

Use It or Lose It

It's illegal in Washington state to advertise for the "restoration of lost sexual potency."

Marriage Is Work, Too

At one time in Hawaii a husband or wife who deserted his or her spouse could be given a month of hard labor. Second offense was a year of hard labor.

Brew Monday

A man and a woman in Northampton, Mass., who owned a restaurant with its own beer brewery found they couldn't get married because it's against the law for close relatives to work in a brewery.

Potty Parity

New York and a handful of other states require that toilets be evenly divided among men and women in public theaters or arenas.

Little Persons' Room

The Santa Monica, Calif., City Council recently proposed that men be allowed to use women's public restrooms when there's a line of three or more at the mens' room, and vice versa.

Miami Vice II

It's illegal in Florida for an unmarried man and woman to live together in "open and gross lewdness." Connecticut once had a similar law, but only the woman was penalized.

Like Driving a Car

You need a license to sell condoms in Washington state.

Too Good for 'em

In the old days in Nevada a man caught beating his wife was tied to a stake for eight hours a day with a sign that read, "Wife Beater" fastened to his chest. In South Carolina, wife beaters weren't allowed to hold public office.

Angel of the Evening

An ordinance in Linden, Ala., provided that all women of "uncertain chastity" had to be off the streets by 9 P.M.

Falsie Alarm

Vietnam veterans may remember that a Vietnamese lawmaker proposed the country should ban the practice of women wearing "falsies." The idea was killed before the lines got too long at the police academy.

Sexist?

A Wisconsin legislator in the 1970s proposed a law providing that no woman over 21 be required to divulge her age. If age information were required by law, women could use an alphabetic code: Women in their 20s would use A, women in their 30s B, and so on. The man who proposed the law would have been a D, had he been a woman and the law passed. He wasn't and it didn't.

Shill No More

A Maryland law outlaws "female sitters," also known as "shills," women paid by owners to sit in their bars and encourage male patrons to buy drinks. Some sitters also worked on commission. The practice was prevalent in a section of Baltimore known as "The Block," where shills would cadge a "champagne cocktail" that would end up costing the sucker who paid for it $20 to $30.

Sidearm

In Missouri male legislators once introduced a resolution urging their female colleagues to strap snub-nosed, .38-caliber revolvers to their ankles.

Book 'em, Dano

In Hawaii a husband or wife who deserted a spouse and failed to reconcile could be given a month of hard labor. Second offense was a year of hard labor.

O Tempora, O Mores

Sodomy laws have been repealed—or are ignored—in most states, but not Georgia, where a man was sentenced not long ago to five years in prison for engaging in oral sex. With his wife. With her consent. In their home. His predicament has apparently been a source of considerable amusement to other inmates.

Wait, Scarlett

An Oklahoma state representative once proposed a bill requiring that a man explain the dangers of pregnancy and obtain a woman's written consent before the two could legally engage in sexual intercourse.

Out of Here

Until 1987 conviction for bigamy in Maryland meant banishment from the state.

You've Come Too Far, Baby

A woman's place is not on a billboard smoking cigarettes, at least in Duluth, Minn., which had an ordinance prohibiting such behavior.

Lady Godiva Need Not Apply

In Columbia, S.C., it's illegal for a woman of "notorious bad character" to ride a horse through town.

Safe Sex

Only registered pharmacists can sell "sex-inciting devices" in Warren, Miss.

Must Be Sick

Under an old Columbus, Ohio, statute, anyone arrested for loitering qualified as a "person suspected of having a venereal disease."

Chapter
IX

No Sleeping at the Wheel and Other Brilliant Legal Insights from the World of Transportation

*saepe viatorum nova, non
vetus, orbita fallit:*

A new road, not an old one, often deceives the traveler.

The Importance of Education

In North Dakota and other states, railroad engineers have to be able to read ordinary handwriting and railroad timetables.

Eat At Joe's

If you see a plane flying a banner over a stadium in Baltimore during a game, the pilot is breaking the law. A 1927 law still on the books makes it illegal to fly a plane "or other flying machine" over a stadium during a game or other event.

Third Boxcar, Evening Train

It is illegal for a hobo to hop a freight through parts of Kansas without the permission of the railroad company.

Keep Arms, Hands, Head, Etc., in the Cab

Several cities, including New York and Youngstown, Ohio, make it illegal for taxis to carry passengers on the outside of the cab. It's dangerous enough inside.

Tarheel Curses

It's against the law to curse aboard a passenger train in North Carolina, but it's OK to let forth with an oath or two on a freight train. It's also against the law to curse on public highways within the hearing of two or more persons, except in two of the state's 100 counties.

A Real Drip

An old law in Green Bay, Wis., put you in violation if your car was dripping fluid on the pavement.

Move That Thing

In Minooka, Ill., it's illegal for a train to stop on any public street for more than 10 minutes at a time.

Hobo Alert

It's against the law in Minnesota for a hobo, or anyone else, to jump onto a moving train. The law doesn't speak to the equally vexing problem of jumping off a moving train.

Move It or Lose It

Minnesota is the land of 10,000 lakes, and the state is bound and determined to keep them open. It's against state law to park a houseboat in front of a public levee.

It Never Lasted Too Long

Early motor vehicle laws in several cities prohibited driving while asleep.

All Aboard

It's illegal in Vermont to throw a snowball at a passing train.

Such a Deal

If a train runs you over in Kansas, state law requires the railroad company to give your remains a free ticket on the train. Bus companies are required to do the same thing.

What's That Up Ahead?

Under Kansas law, a railroad engine has to have a headlight that will "plainly show the figure of a man ... at a distance of 800 feet." The law doesn't apply to trains heading for the repair barn or trains that don't go more than 10 miles into the state.

Of Colts and Mustangs

It took many years for the nation to change from the horse to the car, and while the change went on, it was hard for the remaining horses to adapt. Many states, including Kansas, made it a law that automobile drivers couldn't frighten horses with cars, had to give horses the right of way and had to stop to let horses pass.

And a Draft for the Draft Horse Here

In old San Francisco it was illegal for a man to enter a bar on his horse.

Jump on the Bandwagon

One of the whackiest laws in U.S. history was presented to the nation by the Kansas Legislature in 1903. It is the famous "Political Band-Wagon Law," and it states:

> "Nothing in this section shall be construed as in any way preventing, obstructing, impeding, embarrassing or in any other manner or form infringing upon the prerogative of any political chauffeur to run an automobilious band-wagon at any rate he sees fit compatible with the safety of the occupants thereof, provided, however, that not less than ten nor more than twenty ropes be allowed to trail at all times behind this vehicle when in motion, in order to permit those who

have been so fortunate as to escape with their political lives the opportunity to be dragged to death, and provided further that whenever a mangled and bleeding political corpse implores for mercy, the driver of this vehicle shall, in accordance with the provisions of this law, throw out a lifeline."

This law made the whole country laugh, even after it was repealed in 1929.

Stay to the Right

An old New York motor vehicle law says cars approaching each other from opposite directions have the right of way.

License to Steal

Oklahoma had a license plate that said, "Oklahoma OK," a remembrance from the famous musical, but legislators weren't happy. They debated and debated changing the plate. Finally a legislator rose and suggested, "Oklahoma, the Land of Lakes, Lawyers, Lobbyists and Legislators." After hours of debate, the solons finally settled on "Oklahoma OK!"—the exclamation point satisfied both sides.

Pot Luck

Rhode Island used to have a bounty on potholes. If you found a pothole on a bridge and reported it, and it wasn't repaired in 30 days, you received a $5 a day bounty until it was repaired. There turned out to be more potholes than $5 bills, and the bounty was repealed.

The Redeye Express

Missouri just repealed a law that made it illegal to drive a stagecoach while intoxicated.

Better to Look Both Ways

It's actually the law in Vermont that you have to stay on the right side of a crosswalk when crossing the street. Of course, most policemen will tell you they don't enforce this law, and in fact are happy if people are in sight of a crosswalk when crossing.

Ahoy ... and Scram

In an 1842 law the commander of the fort at Portsmouth, N.H., could stop any ship entering the harbor that had quarantined passengers aboard.

Sounds of Silence

Under Illinois' so-called "boom box act," car radios are not supposed to be heard more than 75 feet from the road.

Call 'em Flyboys

Nevada just went through its laws and changed the word "aeronaut" to "pilot."

Whoa, Nellie

In Nevada it's a misdemeanor to gallop your horse over a covered bridge. This has been the law ever since the days of the Old West. Of course, for many of the persons who had to gallop over a bridge, it was probably what lawyers now call a "lesser included offense."

No Sidewalk Surfin'

Skateboarding has been outlawed in Norwich, Conn.

It's Not a Bird, It's Not a Plane

Louisville, Ky., outlaws hangliding in city parks.

Even the Football Team?

In Maine no one wearing "shoes with spikes" can enter a railroad car without permission of the owner.

View From the Top

In New York City it's illegal, not to mention stupid and dangerous, to ride on top of either a subway car or an elevator car.

Pollution Control
In Charleston, S.C., the horses that pull carriages through the historic streets must wear diapers.

Honk, but Don't Stop
In Christiansburg, Va., it's illegal to stop a vehicle "upon the street at any time for the purpose of advertising."

If They Found You
Under an old Minnesota law you could go to jail for up to 20 years for standing in front of a moving train.

Need an Upgrade
In Canada it's illegal to enter a plane during flight.

Park It, Toots
Nevada has banned "monster" trucks.

And the Roadies
Virginia allowed drivers to drink alcohol while they drove until 1989.

Ptooey
It's illlegal to spit on a bus in the state of Washington.

Caught Speeding
Nevada raised its speed limit to 70 mph, lost federal highway funds, lowered the speed limit and got the money back, all in one morning in 1986. The head of the state's highway department was left with a bunch of unused signs.

Staying Clean
In Arizona it's illegal to tamper with a factory-installed anti-pollution device in your car.

Something to Be Said for It

You can't ride a bike in Washington state unless your bike has a "permanent and regular seat."

Call It Scrap Metal

In New York City a junk boat has to have the words "Junk Boat" painted on the side.

Driving to Distraction

Catch the soaps at home in Washington state, where it's illegal to drive with a TV set in the front seat.

Blessed Mr. Goodwrench®

In Wyoming, a vehicle left unattended by "acts of God or mechanics" is not considered abandoned.

How About the Gun Rack?

In Flossmoor, Ill., it's illegal to park your pickup truck in front of your house or in your driveway.

Passing Fancy

It's illegal to be inside a house trailer in Connecticut while it's moving.

Outta Gas

In Washington state it's illegal to coast down a hill in a car or truck.

Dang Contraption

An old Iowa law required every automobile to stop for a team of horses.

Your Own Risk

Until a few years ago, Connecticut law allowed the state to post roads as being "legally closed," but leave them open to traffic.

Boozer Loser

A new Idaho drunken driving law mandates that three-time offenders display special license plates on their cars.

The Horse Right Here

There were even parallel parking laws in the horse-and-buggy days. An old Danville, Ky., law said all horses attached to vehicles backed to the curb had to be turned to the right. Danville was strict with horses. Another law from the period said anyone operating a merry-go-round within a half-mile of the town had to get a permit. It was also against the law to ride an unbroken horse or to leave a buggy on the street during the Sabbath.

Stinkmobiles

It's against the law of Nicholasville, Ky., to park on the street a vehicle that "emits bad and noxious odors."

Chapter
X

Don't Hang Your Shorts from the Yard and Other Legalities About Dress and Appearance

white gloves:

In ancient courts, when there was no
offender to try, the sheriff would
present the judge with a pair of
white gloves.

As American As Chop Suey

In a burst of jingoism many years ago, the city fathers of Warren,
Idaho, once required that Punch and Judy puppets wear American
clothes.

Hair Today, Gone Tomorrow

The trend toward long hair that began in the late 60s ran right
into a bunch of old laws, and some new ones, against long hair on
men. Cambridge, Mass., for example, had such a law, which
Harvard students broke with abandon. Binghamton, N.Y., made it
illegal for ninth-grade boys to grow moustaches (doubtless taking
the heat off the youngsters who hadn't as yet spouted facial hair).

Please, No Starch

If you're having your shirts done in San Francisco, make sure your laundryman has a spray bottle. It's against the law to spray clothes with water emitted from the mouth.

Something in Peach?

For years, all lifeguards in Georgia were required to wear bright red bathing suits.

You Bought 'em, You Wear 'em

Several Vermont stores have the following sign: "State Law: No Refunds or Exchanges on Underwear." State officials are waiting to see if the law is challenged, because they can't find it anywhere on the books.

Tide's Out

If you go aloft with your skivvies in Key West, Fla., you better be wearing them. It's illegal to hang laundry from a boat tied up at a city dock. Nude sunbathing is also illegal.

Cubist Cap

Drawings accompanying the police and firefighters' grooming ordinance of Covington, Ky., indicate that while hair must be neat and moustaches trimmed, it's apparently OK to have three eyes. Picasso may have been passing through town.

Save Your Shoes

In Fort Wayne, Ind., it's against the law to burn leather as fuel.

These Poils Ain't Cheap

It now costs $1,000 for a license to produce cultured pearls in the waters of Tennessee.

Eye of the Beholder

A former San Francisco ordinance prohibited anyone who was "ugly or grotesque" from going out in public at certain times of the day. Chicago had a similar law, prohibiting anyone "diseased, maimed, mutilated or in any way deformed to be unsightly" from walking about, exposing himself to public view.

Pearl of Wisdom
Between Dec. 1 and Dec. 25 it's illegal to auction jewelry in Wisconsin.

Hot Dog
Zion, Ill., orders all street vendors to be properly attired in "shirts or blouses and shoes." Pants or skirts are optional.

Miami Vice
The sun and fun capital of the world or not, it's illegal in Miami Beach, Fla., to wear a bathing suit on sidewalks, streets or highways unless the suit is covered with a "cloak, robe or other covering from shoulders to knees."

Make Your Point
Nevada law used to prohibit hatpins with a point protruding more than a half-inch beyond the hat. It only applied to hats worn in public places.

Rotten Cotton
Anyone who finds "wrecked cotton" floating on the waters of Florida must advertise the find. This apparently applies to bales of raw cotton, rather than say, shorts.

Grab Your Coat
One Arizona legislator offered a bill that would have made it illegal to appear in public without a sweater or a coat when the mercury dipped below 55 degrees Fahrenheit. It didn't pass.

Speaking of Hats

Secondhand hats offered for sale in Connecticut had to be identified with, what else, block letters.

X-Ray Vision

Superman would have a tough time selling shoes in Washington state, which prohibits fluoroscopic X-ray shoe-fitting devices. This law may be aimed at a device called a "Foot-O-Scope" a chain store used a few years ago.

Chapter
XI

You Chickens Get Out of Town
by Sundown and Other Laws
About Animals

fold-soke:

The feudal requirement that a peasant allow his sheep to lie in the lord of the manor's fold, so the lord could take advantage of the manure.

Dumb Cluck

In Idaho it's illegal to sell chickens after dark without a permit.

Pole Cat

Cats cannot chase dogs up telephone poles in International Falls, Minn. Who is supposed to break this news to the cats?

Hold Your Nose

It used to be against the law to sneeze on the streets of Asheville, N.C. It seems sneezing frightened the horses.

Wagon Train

Visitors to Baltimore know the city has been famous for years for its "street arabs," peddlers who sell food and other things from horse-drawn wagons. A couple of years ago the city council noticed that some of the horses were looking a little down at the mouth, so they decided to do something about it. Now if the temperature gets over 92 degrees Farenheit, or below 20 degrees, the horses have to be taken off the street. They also have to be sent to the barn during snow emergencies.

Sting Operation

America is loaded with laws about bees. In Chicago, for example, it's illegal to keep bees within the city limits. In Connecticut it's against the law to lure bees away from their rightful owner.

I'll Take a Dozen

In Baltimore it's illegal to sell baby chicks within two weeks of Easter in quantities of less than four. This may be a good excuse for parents who aren't thrilled with the idea of a new chirper in the house.

Born Free, More or Less

It is illegal in Baltimore to sell live fowls that are tied by the legs. The crime carries a $2 per-bird fine.

The Goose Thanks You

In California and Kansas it's illegal to pick feathers from a live goose. It's also illegal to trap birds in cemeteries in several states.

Why Did the Chicken ...

In Quitman, Ga., it's illegal for a chicken to cross a public road.

If It Oinks, It's Outta Here

It's illegal to take a pig into a public building in St. Paul, Minn.

They Sound Like Two Animals

It's illegal to watch a dogfight in Denver, but it is legal to watch a cockfight in San Juan, Puerto Rico.

The Dog Gets Life

If you own a dog that has killed either a sheep or a human being, and you don't do anything about it, you're in trouble in North

Carolina. If you let the dog run free, you can be fined up to $50 and put in jail for up to 30 days.

At Least They'd Be Clean

An old borough ordinance in Brooklyn, N.Y., makes it illegal for certain animals to sleep in the bathtub. Hey, not everybody has a spare room. But in Clawson City, Mich., it's OK to sleep with your animals.

Buck Naked

"It is unlawful to take deer swimming, or in water above the knees of the deer," reads a North Carolina law. Does this mean deer have to stay in the hot woods, sweating all summer, until the legislature corrects this obvious oversight? Actually, the law means you can't shoot a swimming deer.

Not Really Stone

Hatteras, N.C., is the one town in the state where a stone-horse or a stone-mule can run wild. How can a stone anything run wild, you might ask. A stone-horse or mule is an old term for an ungelded horse or mule. We're not sure if this had anything to do with the naming of singer Linda Ronstadt's first back-up group, the Stone Poneys.

Rats with Tails

It is against the law for dogs to chase or even worry squirrels on the grounds of the state capitol in Raleigh, N.C.

Civic Porpoise

The city of Malibu, Calif., recently passed a resolution making the city a "Human-Dolphin Shared Environment." The city council vowed to consider the welfare of "local resident" marine mammals as well as migrant mammals, and to improve the relationship between humans and cetaceans. Don't get us wrong. Some of our best friends are marine mammals. We just don't want them on the golf courses.

They'll Just Peck Each Other

In North Chicago, Ill., it's illegal to have more than 25 chickens in any building within the city limits.

Wild, Wild Horses

It's hard to imagine now, but in the early 1700s Pennsylvania had a problem with wild horses. It seems a bunch of horses described as short and ugly were fooling around with the domestic horses, the result being a lot more short, ugly horses. So the colony passed a law creating a ten-shilling bounty on any short, ugly horse that a freeholder could catch and geld. Since no more was heard of the problem, the law apparently worked.

Think How the Bird Feels

It is illegal in Vermont to keep a pigeon to shoot at for amusement.

They Don't Mix

An old Vermont law made it illegal to ship a pig in the same railroad car with a cow. They'll argue over who gets the window, and soon there'll be no living with them.

Want a Cracker, Mate?

Mississippi recently repealed a large body of law having to do with birds of the budgerigar family. There were laws having to do with banding budgerigars, keeping budgerigars in public places, treating sick budgerigars, transporting budgerigars. How these laws got on the books in the first place is anyone's guess. Budgerigars are a kind of Australian parakeet.

No Filet of Fluffy

Michigan is considering an ordinance that will make it illegal to eat domestic cats and dogs. We are not privy to why Michigan is considering such an ordinance.

A Fowl Act

Kansas encourages chicken thieves to do their work during the day. Under the old penal code, chicken stealing at night was grand larceny, while chicken abduction during the day was only petty larceny.

Leapin' Lizards

A 1903 Kansas law makes it illegal to eat, or even pretend to eat, snakes, scorpions, lizards, centipedes "and other reptiles" in public. It's perfectly OK, however, to eat them in private. Or pretend to eat them in private, if that's your inclination.

Goat Herd Ahead

In New York motorists must use due care to avoid goats in the road that are under the supervision of a pedestrian.

Beware the Serpent

A Washington, D.C., City Council member introduced the Snake Amendments of 1983, designed to "control certain peregrinations by snakes" in the city. Under the proposal the mayor was ordered to impound all poisonous snakes except those in the National Zoo. He was also ordered to nab all nonpoisonous snakes except those in the immediate control of their owner in a single-family house. Such an owner could keep his snake, but he would have to post his house with a sign which read, "Snake in House, Exercise Caution." The mayor decided he had better things to do, and the ordinance didn't pass.

Do the 'gator

It is illegal to walk an alligator down the main street of Charleston, S.C. Depending on the temperament of the animal, it may also be unhealthy.

Down, Boy

In Minooka, Ill., it's illegal to encourage two dogs to fight.

Dying to Get Back

According to Alabama law, "all garfish taken by any person in any waters must be killed before returning to the waters of Alabama."

Lassie Come Home

The chief of police of Wingate, N.C., is ordered by law to execute any dog he finds running in heat if he can't find the owner in four days.

Razing Cats and Dogs

The fur flew in Maine a couple of years ago when a legislator proposed a bill legalizing the killing of cats who attack domestic birds. That one didn't pass, but it's legal to blast a dog who gets into a hen house.

No Place for Cat Woman

Anderson, S.C., is a tough town on cats. According to city ordinance, cats aren't allowed anywhere in the city, including the premises of a person who owns a cat.

Home, James

It's against the law in Louisville, Ky., to drive a pig through the streets, unless the animal is in a vehicle.

Am I Glue?

In Connecticut a horse has to get a note from its doctor before it can be auctioned.

For Whom the Bell Tolls

The Miami Beach, Fla., charter used to require that any cat outside a residence or store room wear a bell or bells that could be heard at least 50 feet away. If a policeman or citizen found a cat out without its bells on, it was his duty to kill the animal.

Rice or Wrong?

A few years ago a legislator in Connecticut declared the state must immediately ban the throwing of rice at weddings because, she said, birds ate it and got sick. The proposal died after ornithologists testified that birds not only didn't get sick, some even liked the stuff.

Wait for the Rest Stop

Connecticut forbids a horse from relieving itself in a public waterway. As is so often the case, the law is unclear on who is to break this news to the horse.

No Red Ponies

In Vermont it's illegal to paint a horse. Maybe that's why all the great artists move to Paris.

Easy, Big Fella

To gather alligator eggs in Florida it takes a state license, not to mention a certain amount of nerve. Also, someone who "feeds or entices" a 'gator in the Sunshine State can be fined or jailed, presuming he is able to stand trial.

The Truth, Now

It's also against the law in Florida to use alligators to promote the sale of alligator shoes if the shoes are made from the skins of "other crocodilia."

A Jungle Out There

It's against California law to abuse an elephant (no kidding, it happened at a zoo). In Texas you need a $100 permit to keep a tiger.

Your Intentions, Rover

In Nevada it's illegal for a dog to "worry" other domestic animals.

Cat Seat Belt

A Vermont legislator recently proposed that anyone transporting a cat in an automobile be required to place the feline in a "cat restraining device."

Off-Road Animals

Maine used to have a law making it illegal to lead a bear on a leash on a public highway. Connecticut says you can't lead a bull down a public highway.

A Pig's Life

The city of Broken Arrow, Okla., has terrific zoning for pigs. A city law prohibits the keeping of swine on tracts smaller than seven acres. Robbins, N.C. requires that all pigpens be at least 200 feet from any home, church or school.

What's Up Ahead?

In Berea, Ohio, any animal out after dark has to display a tail light.

Natural Light

New Hampshire law says you're guilty of a misdemeanor if you are a "natural person" and you steal a bear or a deer.

Hare Today, ...

Until recently, if you raised rabbits or Belgian hares in Hawaii, you had to keep them off the ground. It's unclear whether the bunnies were allowed to come down between hops.

Singles Barns

For a cow with a poor social life, Simsbury, Conn., was the place to be. The Board of Selectmen was required to keep eight bulls to service all local cows. Cows are now on their own; the 1714 law was recently repealed.

Make Mine Ribs

Until a few years ago in Arkansas if a pig got into an unenclosed cotton gin and injured itself, the owner of the gin was liable for the pig's injuries.

A Fine Time

If a bitch was found running about in heat in Joliet, Ill., the owner used to be subject to a fine of $1 to $10.

Baaaa

Nevada legislators just repealed a law barring the herding or grazing of sheep within three miles of a post office.

To Bee or Not to Bee

In Lewiston, Maine, it's illegal to keep honeybees in a residential zone. One bee fancier tried to challenge the law on the grounds that his bees were household pets, but he failed.

Kids Today

If your billy goat runs wild in Wisconsin, you've got to pay $5 to the person who finds him.

Anyone Seen Bo Peep?

In Colorado it's illegal for a shepherd to desert or abandon his flock without at least five days notice to the owner.

Even Mr. Ed?

Washington state forbids anyone to steal another's pet animal and sell it to an animal research facility.

A Sparrow Fell

Nevada used to protect songbirds, plume birds and insect-eating birds, but allowed English sparrows to be killed at will.

Noisy Cluck

It's against the law in Duluth, Minn., for anyone to harbor a chicken whose "loud and frequent or habitual crowing or clucking" annoys neighbors or passers-by.

Pigeon's Progress

In Maryland it's illegal to interfere with the flight of a carrier pigeon.

Pigeon's Progress II

In Wisconsin it's a fine of up to $50 for anyone who impedes the progress of a homing pigeon.

Pigeon's Progress III

In Washington state it's illegal for anyone to shoot a racing pigeon except its owner.

Donkey Rule

Washington state also declares that a donkey on the loose is a public nuisance.

Duck the Question

Trespassing by a duck is illegal in Indiana.

Over the Hump

It used to be a $100 fine to let your camel walk down a public street in Nevada.

Cured Pork

All garbage fed to swine in Washington state must be heated to 212 degrees Fahrenheit. Anyone who feeds garbage to swine must have a license.

Old Paint Fainted

In Maine it's illegal to rent a diseased horse.

Go South for the Spring

Chickens aren't allowed to walk around Robbins, N.C., during planting and gardening season.

Cool It, Ferdinand

If a bull gets into a field of cows or heifers in Washington state between March 1 and May 15, the owner of the cows can capture the bull and castrate him.

Don't Spare the Rod

In Kansas it's illegal to catch fish with your bare hands.

All That Glitters

You can't use a goldfish for bait in Connecticut.

Fish in a Big Barrel

In Vermont's Lake Champlain it's legal to shoot pickerel, northern pike and certain other fish with a gun. This law is debated every year, sometimes after a bullet bounces off the water and strikes another fisherman.

Did They Mean Aerobic?

A law in Person County, N.C., prohibits a female dog from running at large "during the erotic stage of copulation." The law doesn't say what the non-erotic stage of copulation is.

Pecking Order

An old ordinance in Columbia, S.C., makes it illegal to carry a chicken through town with its head dangling down. Chickens had to hold their heads high, even if they didn't feel like it.

It Stinks

Since 1894 it's been illegal to boil the entrails of cattle and render up lard within the city limits of Danville, Ky.

Polly, Want a Dry Cracker?

In Connecticut parrots with diarrhea face quarantine.

Love That Dirty Water

It's illegal to throw fish entrails into Boston Harbor. On the other hand, it's illegal to sell most fish on the docks with the entrails still in them.

Faithful Companion

To comply with the state's laws of domicile, retirees who move to Florida are advised to exhume deceased pets and rebury them in their Florida property.

Santa Clause

The 1986 U.S. Tax Reform Act exempted profits from the sale of reindeer.

Tastes Like Chicken

A California legislator recently introduced a bill that would exempt ostrich steaks from the state's sales tax.

Magic Twanger

Solons in Georgia and South Carolina have introduced bills making it illegal to lick a South American cane toad. The toads emit a hallucinogenic toxin.

Chicken Little Was Right Again

A South Carolina legislator has introduced a bill making it illegal to fire a gun within 300 yards of a chicken coop. The noise scares the chickens, said the sponsor of the bill. He said they lose their renowned self-composure, jump into a pile and suffocate one another.

Chicken Who?

Idaho just changed its law that required chicken owners to tattoo their birds.

Chapter
XII

Zany Miscellanies—Laws You Probably Wouldn't Believe

frustra expectatur eventus cujus effectus nullus sequitur:

An event is vainly expected from which no effect follows, or put another way: There's no point in waiting for an event if the event is pointless.

Woodstock, Miss.?

You can be fined up to $20,000 for running a rock festival in Mississippi without a permit. A rock festival is defined as a rock concert that goes on for more than 18 hours. Is there a way for rockers to avoid this law? Yes. Hold the rock festival in a church. Rock festivals in churches are exempt.

A Pointed Exception

It's against the law in Minnesota to form an armed association, such as a terrorist group or a private army. Members of social and benevolent groups are allowed, however, to wear swords.

What Tree, Officer?

In an effort to protect the trees that cover the Green Mountain State, Vermont has a "suspicious tree law." When a police officer sees a vehicle going down the highway carrying a suspicious-looking tree, he can pull the vehicle over and ask to see a bill of sale. If the driver can't produce one, he can be arrested for tree-napping.

Party Hearty

For years in this country people shared telephone lines called "party lines." Now they're all but gone. Nonetheless, you can get an inkling of some of the problems that went along with party lines from a law still on the books in Vermont, which makes it illegal for a person to "declare an emergency to get the line." The phone company is required by law to print the party-line law in the phone book.

Right in the Ice Hole

To avoid sudden surprise for skaters, it's illegal to cut a hole in the ice in Vermont and not put a fence around it.

How About Guard Towers?

It is illegal in Vermont to put a barbed-wire fence around a school.

How Could They Tell?

Vermont recently repealed its law prohibiting the showing of flags that are opposed to organized government.

Something in a Brown

It's illegal in Vermont to paint a utility pole, unless you are the utility and own the thing.

Yellow Peril

In Vermont it's illegal to run a urine farm or sell urine without a state license. Why, you might well ask, would anyone get into this particular line of work? We wondered ourselves. It seems that the urine of pregnant mares contains hormones that can be extracted and used to fight several diseases.

The Final Tab

Back when you could be arrested for being in debt, New York offered a rather gruesome alternative. No police officer could arrest a dead person for being in debt. Now we have kinder, gentler bankruptcy.

Out on a Toot

If you ran a still in Kentucky, you were supposed to equip it with a whistle.

Down to the Bone

A Texas legislator recently tried to introduce Koran justice into the Lone Star State. He proposed that the state cut off parts of the fingers of convicted drug felons, starting with the tip of the finger for the first offense, and on down to the third knuckle. Fearing an Eighth Amendment challenge, as cruel and unusual punishment, the idea was defeated.

A Sterling Performance

In Connecticut it's illegal to make false statements about your silverware if you are going to sell it at auction.

All Aboard

Giving respect where it's due, Kansas still allows Civil War veterans to ride the trains for free. Actually, the law specifies that only Union veterans get free passes. But since the war ended over 125 years ago, any old Reb that happened by would certainly get a senior citizen discount.

Jumpin' Gehozifat

In Kansas from 1877 to 1925 the mayor of any town could, on the request of 15 legal voters, call out all able-bodied men into a "grasshopper militia" to destroy locusts or migratory grasshoppers.

No Smoking

No-smoking laws are hardly new. In 1647, the Connecticut Colony banned all social smoking. A colonist could use tobacco once a day, but not in the presence of other people. The settlers didn't know about lung cancer, but they believed that smoking led to dissipation.

How About a Map?

In Washington, D.C., cab drivers are required to carry a broom and shovel in the trunk. Since the nation's capitol is notoriously bad at dealing with snow, this may be the snow removal program.

Official Calm

It's official policy in Alaska not to get too excited. According to Sec. 44 of the Alaska Statutes, "It is state policy that emergencies are held to a minimum and are rarely found to exist."

I Swear He's Dead

In Nevada it's illegal for a funeral director to use "profane, indecent, or obscene language" in the presence of a dead person. Nebraska and Wyoming have similar restrictions.

Take the Pledge

South Dakota has a new pledge of allegiance: "I pledge loyalty to the flag and state of South Dakota, land of sunshine, land of infinite variety." No one will be forced to recite it.

No Wonder Prisoners Are Angry

The Maryland Legislature passed a bill raising the number of letters allowed on a vanity license plate from six to seven. Somewhere, a fan of the Baltimore Orioles is pleased.

In Marlboro Country ...

Non-Indians face a $10-per-pack fine if they buy cigarettes on an Indian reservation in the state of Washington.

Smelly Bottom

It is illegal to give any place in Maine an offensive name. Maine likes clean names, like Bath.

They Aim to Please

New York state just passed a law reducing the maximum volume of water per flush of a urinal from six gallons to four.

Hit List

A Michigan legislator recently proposed the creation of a "Registry of Bothersome Practices," in which state residents could list things that bother them. Proponents of the bill started the ball rolling with elevator music, subscription cards that fall out of magazines and modular furniture.

Bare Facts

It's illegal to run a nudist colony in Nevada without a permit from the state.

Say, 'Cheese,' and Mean It

It's possible to commit treason against the state of Wisconsin.

B-R-R-R-R-R

In Washington state it's against the law to mislabel or water down antifreeze.

Dive

No skinny-dipping in Boston if you can be seen from a dwelling-house, wharf or street.

Bawk, Cheep, Cheep

Georgia just dropped its sales tax on liquified petroleum gas used to heat chicken coops.

Rambo, Call In

Terrorist organizations are not allowed to train in Idaho.

The Wrong Tree

It's illegal in Washington state to peel cascara bark without a written permit from the owner of the tree.

Dig It

In Boston only registered voters can dig sea worms within the city limits and sell them.

Carry It On

In Washington state it used to be against the law to cause injury to a passenger's baggage. This was repealed, presumably at the request of the major airlines.

Tough Enough to Win

It's still against the law in San Francisco to possess lottery tickets, even though California has a state lottery.

Blue Laws

People in many states know Blue Laws as the laws that kept stores closed on Sundays into the 1970s and 1980s. But actually the laws, so called because they were printed on blue paper, go back to colonial days, and were both stricter and stranger. They included:

- No food or lodging shall be afforded to a Quaker, Adamite or other Heretic.

- No one shall travel, cook victuals, make beds, sweep house, cut hair or shave on the Sabbath.

- Married persons must live together or be imprisoned.

- Every male shall have his hair cut round according to a cap.

- No one shall cross a river on Sunday except an authorized clergyman.

- No one shall make minced pies, play cards, dance, or play on any instrument of music except the trump, trumpet, or jewsharp.

- Anyone who publishes a lie to the detriment of his neighbor shall sit in the stocks or receive 15 lashes.

Put a Cork in It

In Waterville, Maine, it's illegal to blow your nose on the street.

Who's on First?

Under an old Washington law, the owner of a grist mill had to help carry grist in and out of the mill if the owner of the grist was unable to do it.

Lowdown Stogies

If you're making stogies in Wisconsin, stay on the first floor or above. The state bans the production of cigars in a basement.

Save Your Confederate Money

If the South rises again, Florida is ready. State law still entitles veterans of the Confederate Army to a pension of $900 a year, even though the last of the Johnny Rebs went to that Big Plantation in the Sky in 1959.

Stars and Bars

With all the recent furor over flag burning, it's good to note that it's been illegal in Florida to mutilate a Confederate flag for more than a century.

Clean Sweep

In Wisconsin water or moist sawdust must be spread on the floors of railroad stations, schools, public buildings, hotels and department stores before they're swept with a broom. Indiscriminate sweepers risk a fine of $10 to $50.

Comic Horror

California law prohibits "tying arrangements" with horror comic books. That means merchants can't require that someone buying a book or magazine also buy a horror comic book.

You Can Answer the Door on Sunday

Wisconsin doesn't allow sheriffs or bill collectors to come after you on Sunday.

Fickle Sickle

The Iowa Senate in 1917 passed a resolution praising the Russians for throwing off the yoke of the czar and pledging them the wholehearted support of Iowa. Two years later Iowa legislators began passing anti-communism measures.

Such a Deal

Any contract made while flying over the state of Wisconsin is valid anywhere in the state.

Dutch Treat

In 1988 Utah's legislators passed a joint resolution "acknowledging the historic role played by the Dutch oven in the development of Utah's families."

Dam Laws

In Connecticut you can legally build a dam if you are: a duly licensed and authorized producer of hydroelectric power; or a beaver.

Step Right Down

For years it was illegal to have a circus in Minnesota within 18 days of the annual state fair.

No Dances with Wolves

Until a few years ago it was illegal in North Dakota to have a dance with the lights turned down low or to invite someone "of known immorality."

He's Only Sleeping

The law forbids a dead person from serving on a jury in Oregon.

Stiff Penalty

Until 1975 in Maine a cop couldn't arrest a dead body.

Mizzen Mast Is Mizzen

The Connecticut legislature recently voted to commission the H.M.S. Rose, a reproduction of a British sailing ship, in the state's naval militia. The state has no naval militia.

Sin Tax

Arizona law requires a person who sells marijuana to obtain a license and pay luxury taxes.

Dueling Bozos

If you want to fight in Nevada, take it outside. It's illegal to hold a duel in a bar. (This frontier-era law is still on the books, we're told, because of the conduct of certain legislators in a Carson City watering hole).

Why Not Tax It?

In Maine anyone who makes, transports, or sells fertilizer must pay a tax of 12 cents a ton. Such a tax in Washington, D.C., could, of course, wipe out the national debt.

Take Some Home

Horse manure found on a public highway in Connecticut is deemed public property.

Use a Pocket

In Washington it's a violation of environmental protection laws to leave a worm can in the woods.

And It Excited the Bull

Due to the "Red Scare" after World War I, it became illegal to display a red flag in several states. Black flags were also banned.

Even At Football Games?

Until 1981 it was illegal to display a flag with an inscription antagonistic to the the state of North Dakota.

Make Up Your Minds

For some reason, Indiana has two state flags.

Great Escape

Hotels in Arkansas, except those with iron fire escapes, are required to have ropes capable of holding 500 pounds and knotted every 15 inches running from each room window to the ground.

Have a Ball

It's illegal for three or more masked or disguised people to gather in Washington, unless they're having fun.

Official State Whatever

Every state has an official flower, motto, song, insect, animal, flag, rock and hero. Some states have gone to extremes:

- Paxton Series soil is Massachusetts' official state dirt.

- A Georgia legislator has proposed that "Tutti-Frutti" by native son Little Richard be the official state rock 'n' roll song.

- A recent New Jersey proposal would make hadrosaurus foulkii the state dinosaur.

- Alaska's official fossil is the woolly mammoth.

- Arizona's official neckware is the bolo tie.

- The Plott Hound is the official dog of North Carolina.

- Illinois' state fossil is the Tully Monster, Tullimonstrum gregarium, which was about a foot long, had a snout like an elephant, and is 300 million years old.

- Georgia's official reptile is the gopher tortoise.

- Oklahoma's state poem is "Howdy, Folks."

- Massachusetts' official beverage is cranberry juice.

- Connecticut's state insect is the praying mantis.

Send Us Your Rich, Etc.
It used to be against the law to import a poor person into the state of Washington. In earlier times you had to be bonded by a resident to be able to move into Newport, R.I.

Four Walls an Elevator Make
Nebraska jails with elevators must, by law, have conductors to operate the elevators.

Whipping Boys
Some Delaware legislators recently proposed that those convicted of serious drug offenses be given five to 40 lashes with a whip on a bare back.

Last Shot
An Oklahoma legislator recently proposed that death row inmates have the option of dying the way their victims did. The Legislature decided to stick with lethal drug injections.

Rodent Power

The governor of Indiana is authorized to declare "Rat Day" every year to advocate control of vermin.

It Looked Like Lettuce ...

In New Hampshire it's illegal to collect seaweed at night.

Flag Phobia

It used to be illegal in Minnesota to possess black or red flags.

Melancholy Baby, OK

In Florida it's illegal for local schoolboards to prohibit the playing of "Dixie."

If They Caught You

In Baltimore spitting from a streetcar used to mean a 50-cent fine.

Hey, Sometimes It Worked

In Hawaii it used to be illegal to attempt to cure someone through means of sorcery, witchcraft, anaana, hoopiopio, hoounauna, hoomanamana, or other superstitious methods.

Snath of Least Resistance

Riding down a highway, lane or street in Maine with a naked scythe, sharpened and hung in a snath, used to be punishable by a $2 fine.

You Listening, Iowa?

It's a felony to wage war against the state of Wisconsin.

Trickery, OK

It's a felony to advocate the overthrow of the Washington state government by force or violence.

Use the Can

You can be fined 50 cents in Washington for wantonly destroying a beer bottle.

Even on Basin Street

It's illegal to gargle in public in Louisiana, according to an old, oft-cited and completely ignored health regulation.

Fragrant Vagrant

In Seattle in the old days anyone found living in an outhouse was considered a vagrant.

Rough Rider

In Wisconsin it's illegal to wear the insignia of the United Spanish War Veterans. Even faking it would be impressive now; the war took place in 1898.

Pilgrim's Progress

In Massachusetts it's illegal to dig up the state flower, the Mayflower, naturally.

Leave It at the Drive-in

In Washington it's illegal to embrace while driving.

But It's a Cream Puff

In Wyoming it's illegal for a funeral parlor operator to bury a body in a used casket.

Cruel and Most Unusual

An obscure Oklahoma law allows a sheriff to walk into the cell of a prisoner on death row and shoot him, if no reason exists to delay the execution.

Make Up Your Mind

It used to be illegal in Florida to stay in the voting booth for more than five minutes.

...and This

A Connecticut education regulation says there are 60 minutes in an hour.

Rags to Riches

It is a misdemeanor in Washington to sterilize wiping rags without first obtaining a registration number.

Michael Jackson, Stay Home

No "immoral, indecent, suggestive or obscene" dancing is allowed in the state of Washington. Also, you need a license to run a public dance.

But My Name Is John Doe

In New Hampshire it's illegal to register at a hotel under a fictitious name.

You Could Give Me a Shine?

In a blow to free enterprise, it's illegal in Atlanta to shine shoes for money on the street.

I've Always Said That

One of California's "maxims of jurisprudence" states: "Superfluity does not vitiate."

Ahead of Its Time?

Iowa banned the sale of cigarettes in 1896 and kept the law on the books for 25 years.

Some Guy Left It Here

The state of Washington makes it a misdemeanor to be in possession of a stolen or "hot" shopping cart.

How Could They Tell?

It used to be against the law in Minnesota to wear the symbol of the Odd Fellows, unless you were an Odd Fellow.

Name That Tune

Under an old Miami law, jugglers, fiddlers and "common pipers" were considered vagrants.

Tomb It May Concern

Under an old Minnesota law, anyone who opened a road through a cemetery without the owner's permission was subject to a $300 fine.

Jim Crow Did Go, Finally

Racist laws were on the books in this country for a long time. First there was slavery. Then "Jim Crow" laws, such as those in Irondale, Ala., which prohibited whites and blacks from such activities as playing together or riding in a taxi at the same time. One of the last such laws was a Nevada statute that said, "Chinamen or Mongolians" couldn't be hired as state employees. It was repealed in 1959.

Spittin' Image

An old Wisconsin law required that cuspidors be put in all public places.

Honest Living

In Alabama you can't obtain a mortician's license through bribery.

It's Not Good for You, Anyway

The tobacco industry has known some very sharp traders over the years—too sharp for law enforcement authorities. So tobacco states such as North Carolina have laws to prevent three types of swindles by tobacco traders. It's against the law to sell nested, shingled or overhung tobacco. What, you wonder, does this mean?

- Overhung tobacco wasn't out drinking last night. The term refers to the arrangement of a pile of tobacco so there are alternating bundles of "good" and "sorry" tobacco.

- Shingled tobacco is arranged so the better-quality tobacco is on the outside and the cheaper, lesser stuff is on the inside, rather like a "Boston bankroll," a roll of bills with a big bill on the outside and small bills in the middle.

- Nested tobacco is tobacco arranged in a pile so that a buyer cannot possibly pull a leaf out from the bottom to inspect it. (This law reminds us of an old joke about an Army parade, in which the Colonel screams, "Why are all the tall men marching up front?" and the major answers, "It's the captain's fault, sir. He used to work in a grocery store.")

We Just Want to Talk to Him

California has a law making it illegal to offer "Wanted: Dead or Alive" rewards for suspects. The law is fairly recent. The "Wanted: Dead or Alive" posters kept a number of bounty hunters in business in the early West.

Punishment Fits the Crime

In Maine it's against the law to throw a bottle cap on the ground. But a judge recently ruled the crime was only worth a fine of five cents, which the guilty party could raise by redeeming the bottle for recycling.

For One Thing, It's Hot

If you buy a spa, pool or hot tub in the state of Washington, the seller is required by law to provide you with information about the health effects of hot water.

Go to a Movie Instead

If William Tell showed up in Minnesota and tried his legendary bow-and-arrow shot, he'd be arrested. It's illegal to have exhibits that involve aiming sharp objects at targets mounted on people. It's also illegal in Minnesota for acrobats to work without a net.

Molly Makes Minneapolis

Minnesota just repealed its ban against the showing of blue movies by drive-in theaters.

Hot Dispute

If a fireman in Montgomery, Ala., tells you to leave a burning building, you have to leave. It's the law. You can't offer any excuse to stay.

Take That, Your Honor

It is illegal to spit on the courthouse floor in Minooka, Ill.

Well-Rounded Man

Although phrenology, a system of analyzing character by studying the shape of the head, has long been discredited, you can still practice it in Trenton, N.J., as long as you get a license from the city and pay a fee.

Memorable Incision

The seat of Danville, Ky., contains a caduceus, a medical symbol, to commemorate the world's first ovariotomy, performed in the city in 1809 by Dr. Ephraim McDowell upon Mrs. Jane Todd Crawford.

Sweet Science

Under a new California law, you literally must have your head examined—for susceptibility to chronic brain damage—before receiving a professional boxing license.

Psst! Want Some Cough Drops?

In Whiting, Ind., it's illegal to give free samples of medicine to anyone under 14, but apparently it's OK to sell it to them.

Don't Call Your Office

In Dallas, lawyers aren't allowed to bring cellular phones into the courtroom.

Masks Too?

In California a lawyer can wear any kind of wig or hat he wants in the courtroom, unless the the presiding judge can come up with a good reason to order him to take it off.

I Just Like the Hat

Until recently it was illegal in Nebraska to impersonate a firefighter.

How About the Hat?

Until the 1950s, lawyers couldn't argue before the South Carolina Supreme Court unless they wore black coats.

Bath Is a Four-letter Word

Physicians used to think, a century and a half ago, baths were unhealthy on the theory that people would get chilled and get ill. So bath taking was regulated. You couldn't take one on Sunday in Boston. In Portland, Ore., you had to wear clothing of some kind. One Indiana town, Clinton, discouraged bath taking all winter. In Minneapolis, bathtubs had to have legs.

Ten-Hut!

Arizona has a Code of Military Justice, for some reason, that says a sentinel or lookout found drunk or asleep on guard duty, in time of war, can be punished by death. Luckily, Arizona doesn't go to war that often.

Life Was Cheaper

An old law in Mississippi exonerated someone who accidently killed his servant, as long as he was in the process of lawfully correcting the servant. An old Vermont law let a cop off the hook for killing a rioter, as long as it was done in the quelling of the riot.

They Want You to Get a Job

An old law in Washington state says healthy people cannot beg for alms.